For information, please contact:
MaryRose Lovgren
P.O. Box 6962, Chico, CA, 95927

Visit the author on the web at:
www.LittleMessyIllustration.com

ISBN-13: 978-1536966213
ISBN-10: 1536966215

This book is dedicated to my husband Ken,
who always believed in me and my art.

CREATURES ~of the~ MYSTERIOUS DEEP

Original Illustrations and Zoological Facts regarding Nine Elusive Dwellers of the Sea

Written and Illustrated by
by MaryRose Lovgren

Note from the Author

After shamelessly browsing the Internet looking at octopus photographs, I was struck with the notion that each image could have been shot not in the deep sea but in outer space. The little specks of dust and debris lit up by the camera's flash could just as easily be the stars in the heavens.

With this inspiration, I set out to create illustrations of nine of these magnificent sea creatures with backdrops that give the illusion of swimming through either flecks of deep sea flotsam and jetsam or clusters of stars.

I included characteristic traits about each organism next to each illustration so that you might draw connections between yourself and these strange, beautiful animals. In fact, you might take the "Personality Quiz" to determine which "Creature of the Deep" you most resemble.

I hope that these drawings and facts prompt you to further explore each incredible animal.

- MaryRose Lovgren

What kind of Creature of the Deep are YOU?
A Personality Quiz

1. My favorite gift to receive is:
    a. A book
    b. A game
    c. A trip
    d. I hate gifts

2. My favorite movie is:
    a. *12 Angry Men*
    b. *Wall-e*
    c. *It's a Wonderful Life*
    d. *The Shining*

3. My favorite flavor of ice cream is:
    a. Vanilla
    b. Bubble Gum
    c. Chocolate Mint
    d. Black Licorice

4. At parties, I:
    a. Carefully mingle
    b. Am the life of the party
    c. Quietly glide around the room
    d. Hide, and then jump out and scare people

5. For fun, I:
    a. Hold lengthy discussions about esoteric topics
    b. Play games with my friends
    c. Enjoy physical activity in nature
    d. Hide, and then jump out and scare people

Now, add up how many a, b, c and d answers you selected and then turn to the next page...

Congratulations! If you picked...

Mostly a:
Your sea spirit animals are the <u>Octopus, Squid, and Nautilus</u>. You are wise, thoughtful and enjoy intellectual stimulation. You love math, especially logarithms. You *might* also squirt ink at people when you get nervous.

Mostly b:
You identify most closely with the <u>Axolotl and Tardigrade</u>. You are young at heart, a little silly and pretty darn cute. Those who don't know you sometimes say you're immature, but that's just because you never developed gills. You *might* also be immortal.

Mostly c:
You would enjoy sea life as a <u>Whale Shark or Ray</u>. You are often described as calm, cool and collected. You make everything look easy as you move effortlessly through space. Everyone wants to hang out with you. Just make sure you don't accidentally eat them.

Mostly d:
You would find comfort as an <u>Eel or Anglerfish</u>. You are unusual and exotic. Your tastes are unique and you are not easily amused. Also, parts of you have been known to glow. Just keep the whole frightening-people-to-death thing to a minimum.

Octopus

An octopus is a cephalopod (meaning "head-foot"), and like all other cephalopods, it has a distinct head, a crushing, parrot-like beak, a mantle and multiple pairs of arms. Octopuses are probably best known, however, for having eight arms covered in sensitive suction cups that can actually taste their surroundings. An octopus has no internal or external skeleton, giving it the ability to squeeze through incredibly small spaces no larger than the size of its beak.

Octopuses are among the most intelligent of all invertebrates. They have numerous strategies for defending themselves against predators, including the expulsion of ink, an incredible use of camouflage and the ability to jet quickly through the water. They can use tools and sometimes carefully arrange shells in a "garden" around their lair.

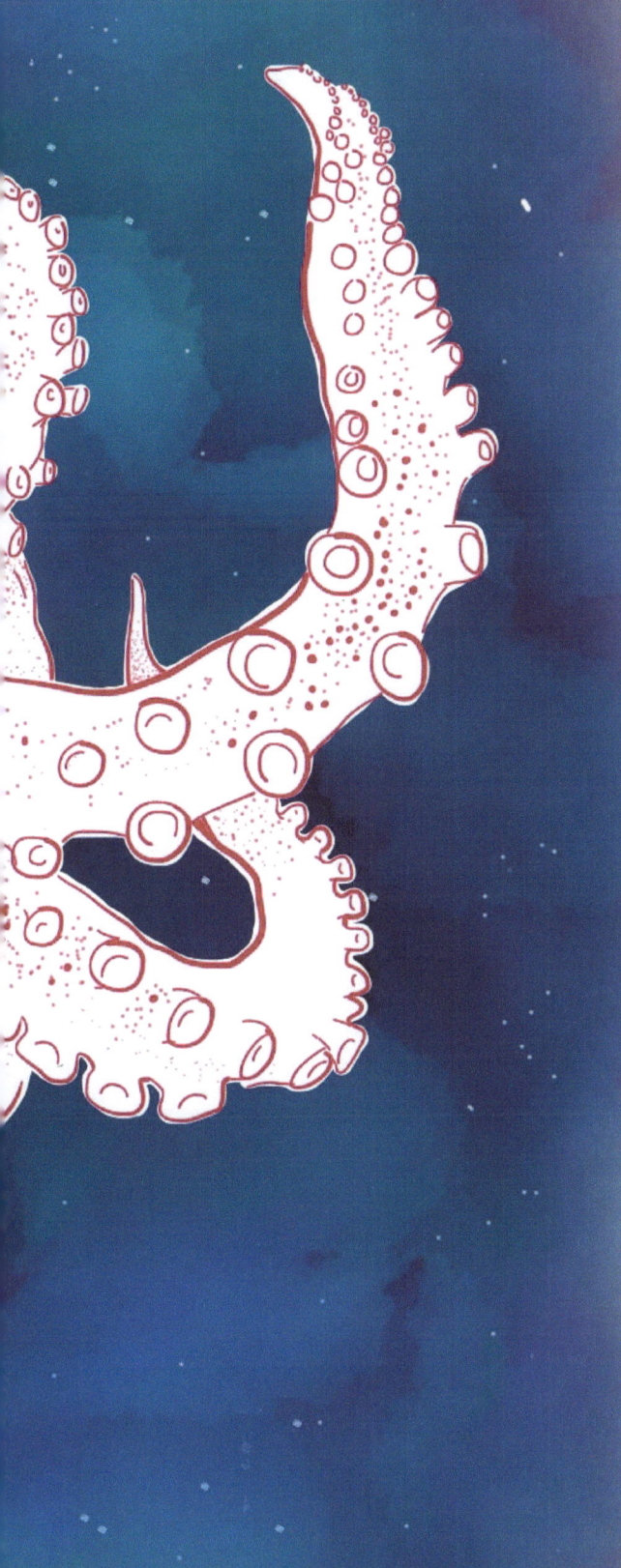

Squid

Squid are cephalopods of the order Teuthida, which comprises about 304 species. Squid, like cuttlefish, have eight arms arranged in pairs and two typically longer tentacles.

The Giant Squid lives up to its name, growing to recorded lengths of 43 feet. Yet despite their size, they remain elusive-- they prefer the deep ocean, and so are rarely seen. Their skin is also covered in cells called "chromatophores" that allow them to change color and camouflage themselves, making them virtually invisible. Sadly, most of what we know about these giants only comes from those who have expired and floated to the surface.

Nautilus

The nautilus (from the Latin form of the Greek word for "sailor") is the sole living cephalopod whose bony body structure is externalized as a shell. Unlike a snail's shell, the nautilus only lives in the outermost chamber; the rest are filled with gas to allow it to be buoyant. The nautilus can withdraw completely inside, closing the opening of its shell with a hood formed from two specially folded tentacles. Its shell is also the finest example in nature of a logarithmic spiral.

The body shape and structure of the Nautilus has changed so little over millions of years that they are considered "living fossils."

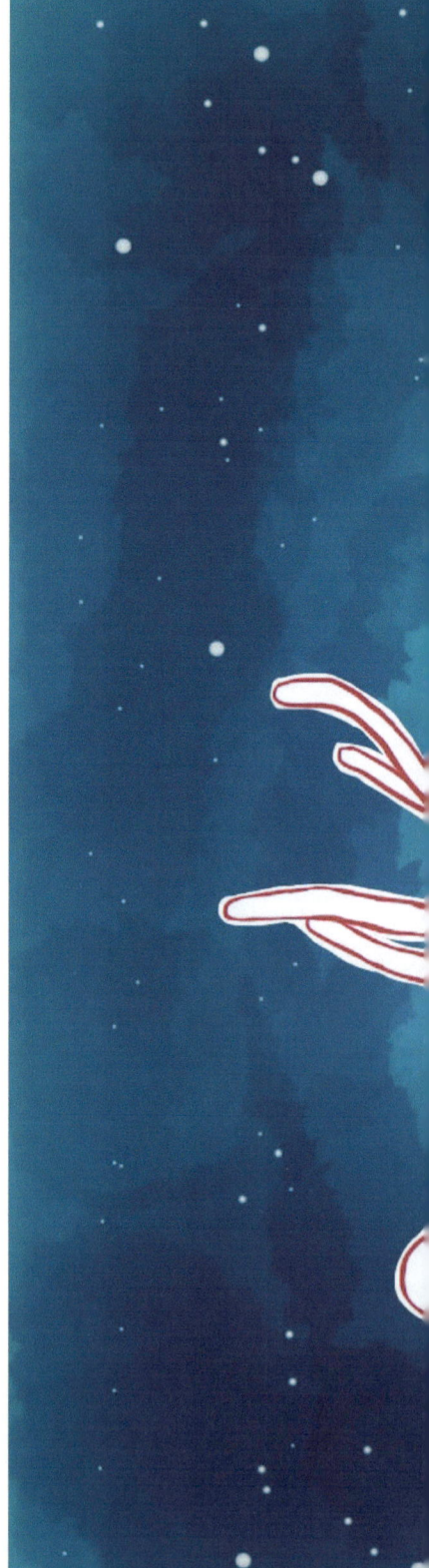

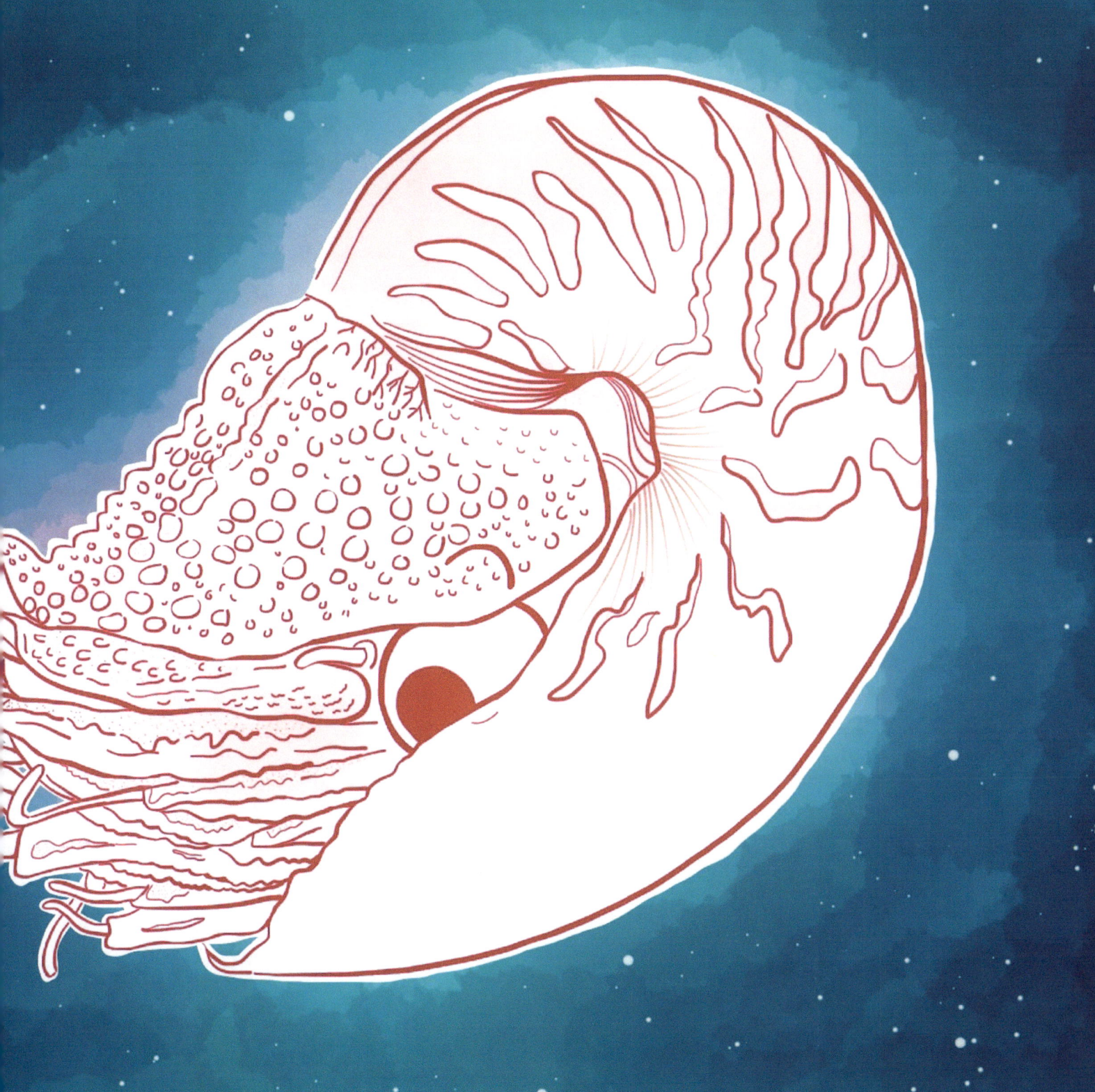

Tardigrade

Tardigrades (also known as water bears or moss piglets) are water-dwelling, eight-legged microscopic animals. They have been found everywhere, from the highest of mountaintops to the deepest parts of the sea.

Tardigrades can survive in extreme environments, including temperatures from just above absolute zero to well beyond the boiling point of water; pressures about six times greater than those found in the deepest ocean trenches; ionizing radiation at doses that would be lethal to a human; and the deadly vacuum of outer space. They can go without food or water for more than 10 years, able to then rehydrate and go about their business again.

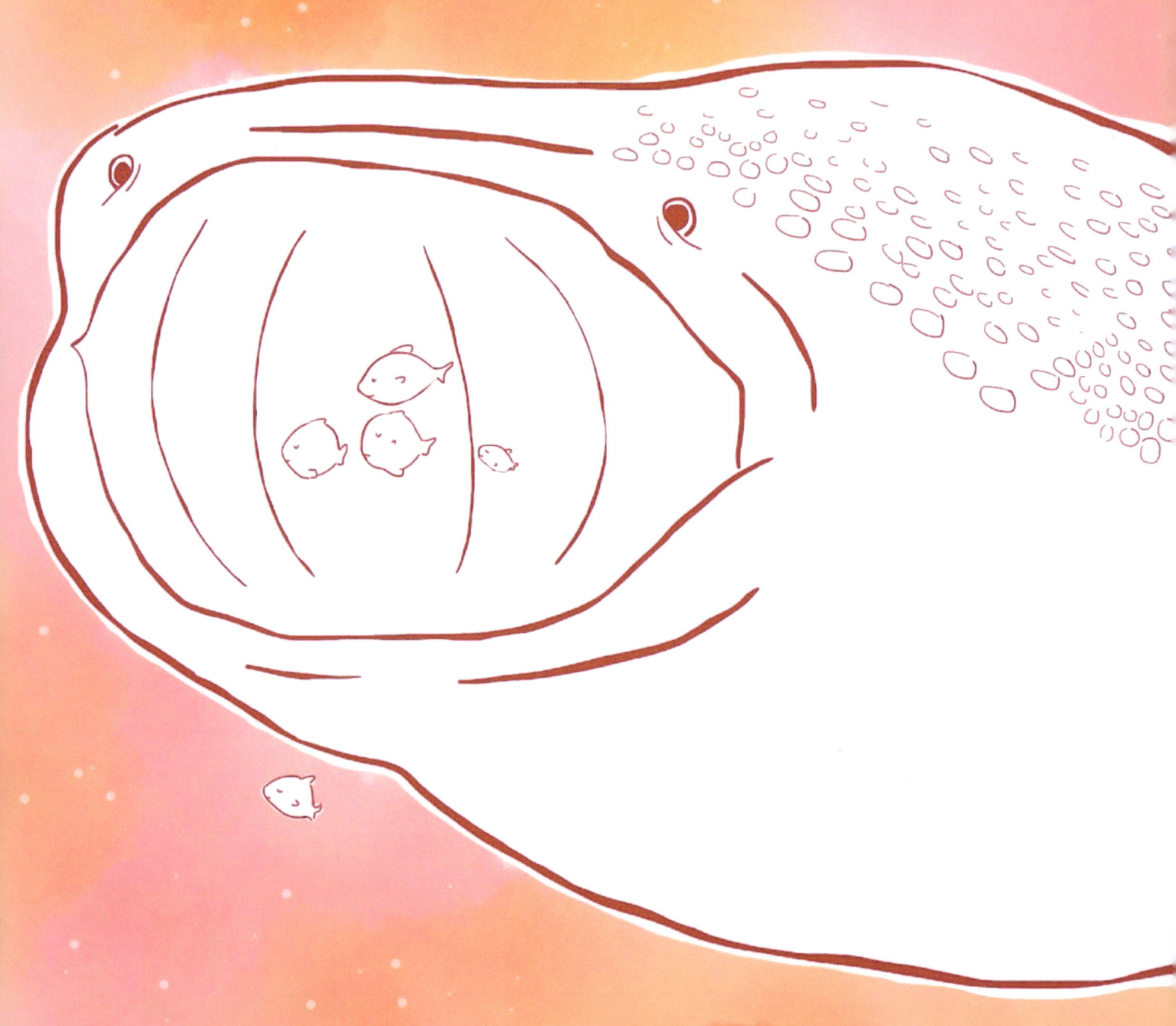

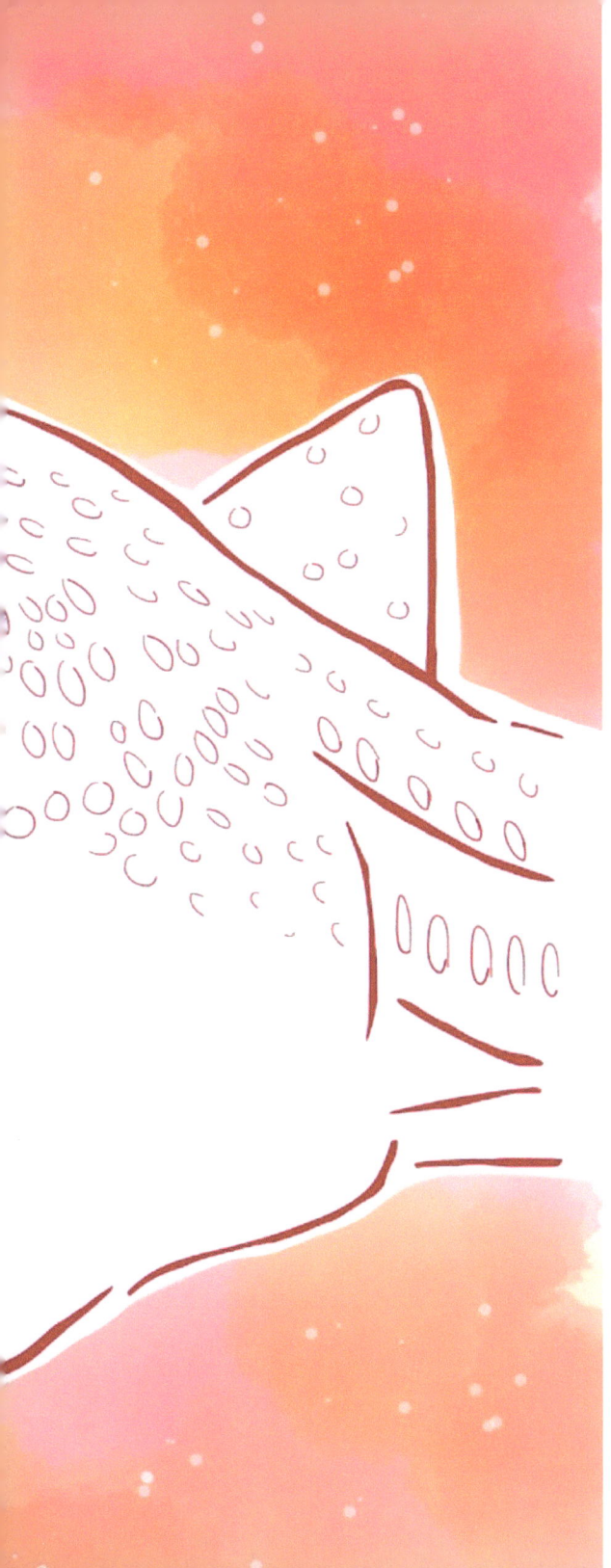

Whale Shark

The whale shark is not only the largest known fish species still in existence, it is by far the largest living vertebrate that isn't a mammal. One whale shark is said to have been over 40 feet long and weighed as much as a fully occupied Greyhound bus. There are unconfirmed reports of even larger ones.

Being so large, whale sharks also have very large mouths, which they use to feed on the smallest organisms in the ocean: Plankton. A whale shark "sucks in" water that is then strained through filter pads, allowing it to trap and then dine on thousands of tiny free-floating plants and animals.

Despite their size, whale shark are gentle creatures. They have even been known to play and swim along with human divers.

Axolotl

The axolotl is an animal with a wide head and distinct fluffy gill stalks. Although the axolotl is colloquially known as a "walking fish," it is not a fish but an amphibian. Axolotls are *neotenic*, meaning they retain the features of its juvenile state as an adult, an unusual trait among amphibians. Instead of developing lungs and moving onto land as it undergoes metamorphosis, the adults retain a tadpole-like aquatic stage and continue to breathe using gills.

The species is native to two lakes in Mexico City; one no longer exists, and the other has been greatly reduced in size. Axolotls are now a critically endangered species, and wild axolotls are nearly extinct.

Eel

An eel is any fish belonging to the order Anguilliformes, which consists of about 800 different species. Eels are elongated and snake-like, with fins that are fused together forming a single ribbon running along the length of their body. Eels can range in size from a couple of inches to a dozen feet (like the slender giant moray eel). They swim by generating waves with their body. They can even swim backwards by alternating the direction of the wave.

Most eels live in the shallow waters of the ocean and hide in caves and rock crevices so that they can spring out to surprise their prey. Eels have been seen living together in holes called "eel pits." When they want to breed, however, some travel as far as 4,000 miles, which is about the length of the Great Wall of China.

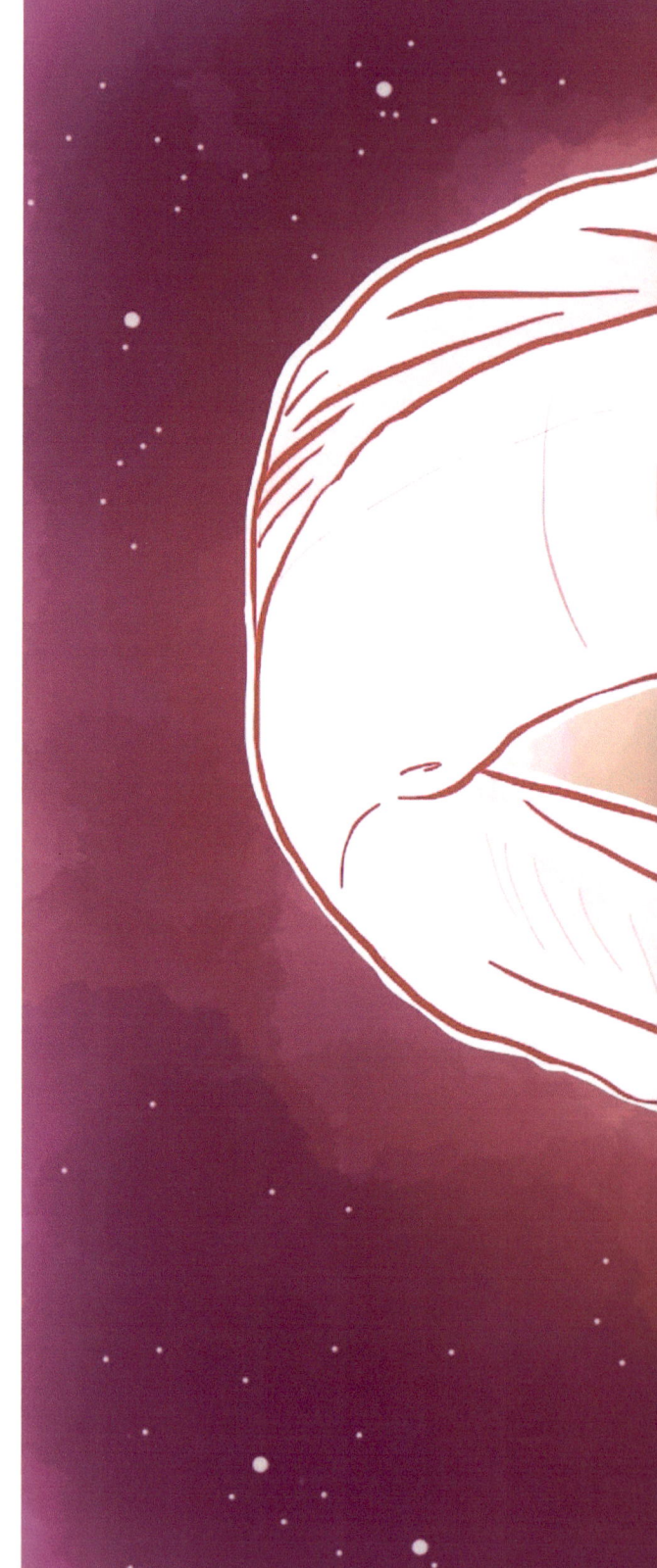

Ray

Rays are members of the superorder Batoidea (which includes stingrays and electric rays), so named because these cartilaginous fish often resemble bats. Rays are distinguished by their flattened bodies, overly large pectoral fins that are fused to the head and gill slits on their ventral (underside) surfaces. Manta rays can be quite large, reaching a wing span of up to 23 feet. A large oceanic manta ray might weigh in at over 4,000 lbs.

Rays are *demersal* (from the Latin *demergere* which means "to sink"), living on or near the bottom of the sea. While rays tend to live alone, they can be curious and social animals and like swimming with others of their species. But watch out for their long, whip-like tail--some come equipped with a poisonous spine.

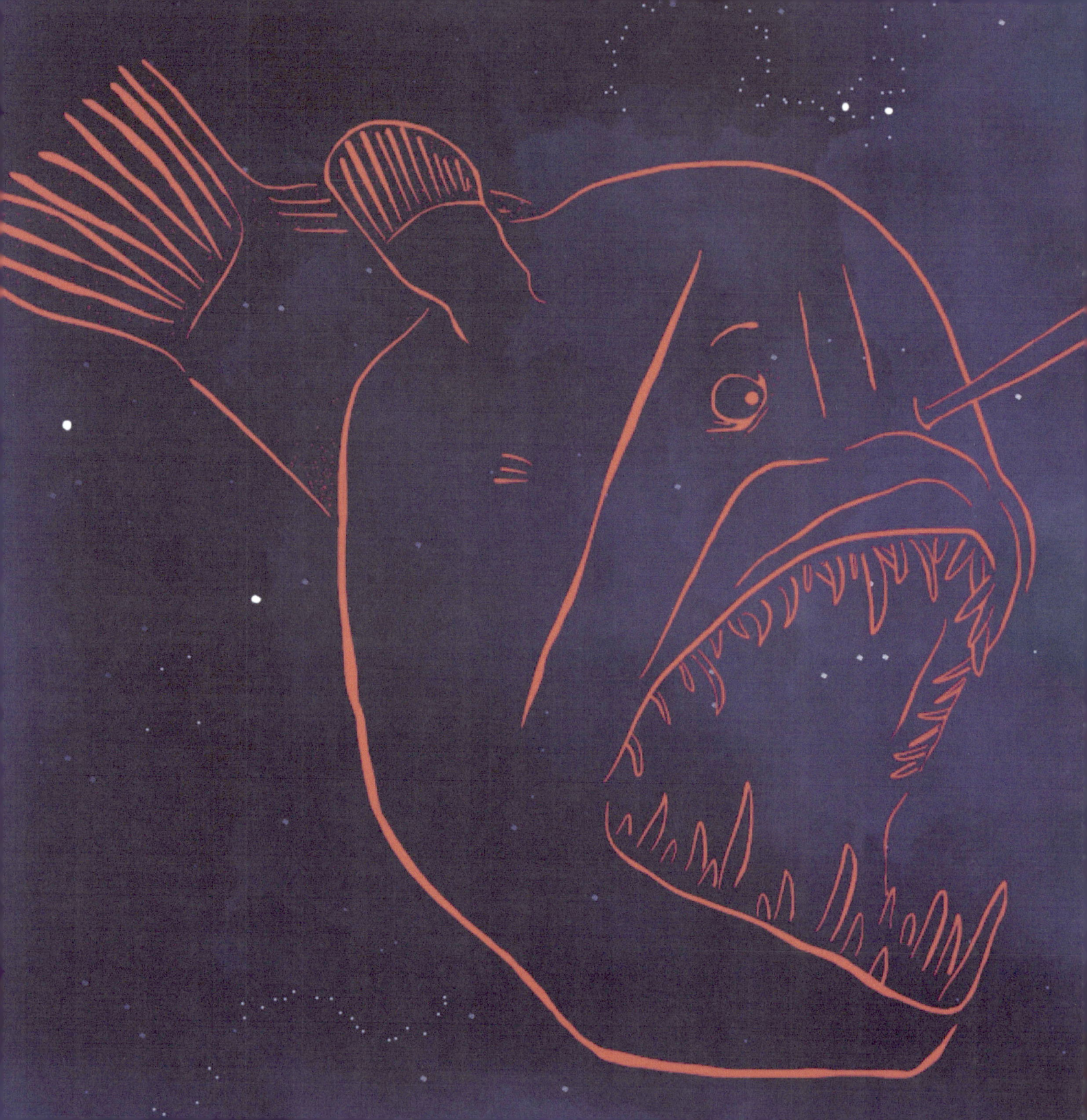

Anglerfish

Anglerfishes are bony fish named for their characteristic mode of predation: A luminescent growth from the tip of their head acts like a fishing lure. (The word "angler" refers to someone who fishes with a rod and a line). Ranging in color from dark gray to dark brown, these carnivores have huge heads and gigantic mouths full of fang-like teeth that angle inward to better grab their prey. An anglerfish is able to swallow prey up to twice as large as its entire body, thanks to its ability to distend both its jaw and stomach.

When a male anglerfish finds a female, he attaches himself to her body and they physically fuse together. This ensures that when she is ready to spawn, he'll already be "hanging around."

About the Author

MaryRose Lovgren has degrees in Zoology and English Literature from the University of California at Davis and uses her background in science and storytelling in her art. She has a fondness for pen-and-ink drawing and the illustrations in children's storybooks. She wouldn't mind living at the bottom of the ocean, although deep-sea anglerfish do make her nervous.

Find more at
www.LittleMessyIllustrationcom